Sophie

about Baptism

Illustrated by
Lula Guzmán

ebby Bradley

Dedication

Grateful
for love and support from my husband, Bill,
and children Claire Marie, Teman John Kaiser,
and Molly Renee.

Blessed
to have as my first religious examples
Fr. Bill Vos and Ade Ledermann.

Thankful
to have witnessed the inspiration of these who have
joined the communion of saints: Kenneth Besetzny,
Judith Batton, Helen Marais, and John Kaiser.

Imprimi Potest:
Harry Grile, CSsR, Provincial
Denver Province, The Redemptorists

Published by Liguori Publications
Liguori, Missouri 63057

To order, call 800-325-9521
www.liguori.org

p ISBN: 978-0-7648-2347-3
e ISBN: 978-0-7648-6885-6

Liguori Publications, a nonprofit corporation, is an apostolate of The Redemptorists.
To learn more about The Redemptorists, visit Redemptorists.com.

Printed in the United States of America
18 17 16 15 14 / 5 4 3 2 1
First Edition

There once was a little girl.
Her name was Sophie.
Sophie wondered about many things.

Today Sophie wondered about
a photograph that showed
a baby in church.

"What are they doing to that baby?"
she asked.

"That's you, Sophie, on the day you were baptized," said Mommy.

Sophie asked, "What is *baptized*?"

"That's when you become a
member of a special family."

"But I already had a family,"
said Sophie.

9

"Yes, but baptism gave you another family—your Christian family.

That's a great big family, honey," her mom explained.

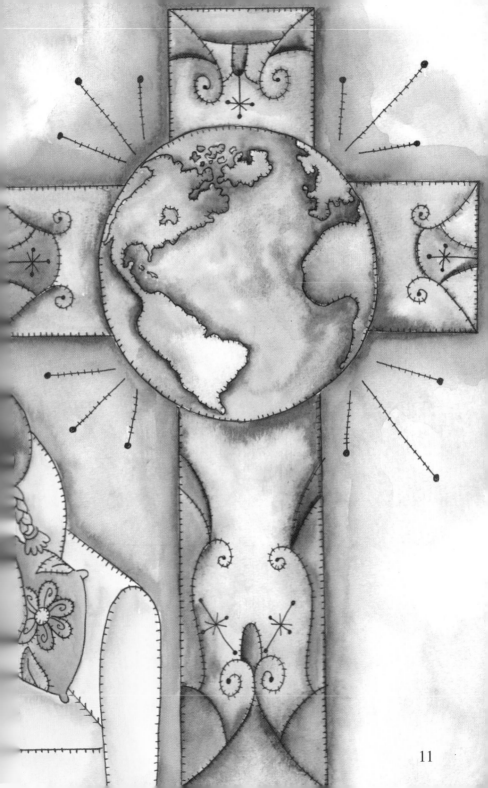

"What is *Christian*?" Sophie wondered.

"A Christian is a person who believes
Jesus is God's son."

"Jesus?" Sophie got excited.
"Do you mean the Jesus we pray to
at bedtime and when we eat?"

"Yes, that's right, Sophie."

Mommy had told Sophie that Jesus was the nicest man ever, and that God sent Jesus to teach us how to love one another.

"Daddy and I try to live just like
Jesus did, and we want to teach
you to live like Jesus too.
That's why we had you baptized.

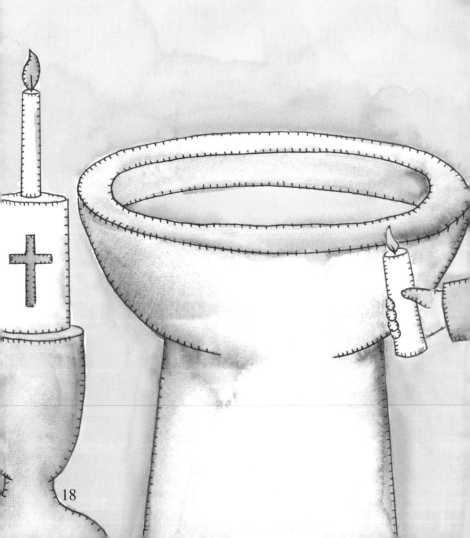

"The priest poured holy water over your head and used his finger to draw a cross on your forehead.

"We lit a candle and then said
a special prayer.

"Everyone in the church
listened and was excited."

Sophie got excited just hearing about it.
"Can I get baptized again?"

"No, Sophie, you can be baptized only one time. But that's all it takes to make you a member of the Christian family forever!"

Sophie smiled.

"That's good news!"

"That's right.
That's exactly what
we call it, honey."

Sophie was so excited she ran off
to "baptize" her dolls.

Sophie Wonders About the Sacraments

To order, visit Liguori.org
or call 800-325-9521